# Population

## Growth

Rufus Bellamy

amicus

Published by Amicus
P.O. Box 1329, Mankato, Minnesota 56002

Printed in the United States of America at Corporate Graphics, in North Mankato, Minnesota.

Published by arrangement with the Watts Publishing Group Ltd., London.

Library of Congress Cataloging-in-Publication Data
Bellamy, Rufus.
  Population growth / by Rufus Bellamy.
      p. cm. -- (Sustaining our environment)
  Includes index.
  ISBN 978-1-60753-137-1 (library binding)
  1.  Population--Juvenile literature. 2.  Overpopulation--Juvenile literature.  I. Title.
  HB883.B45 2011
  304.6'2--dc22

                                                    2009030032


Series editor: Adrian Cole
Art Director: Jonathan Hair
Design: Simon Borrough
Picture Research: Diana Morris

Acknowledgements:
Aerial Archives/Alamy: 26l. Affordable Housing Institute: 18. G M B Akash/Panos: 35. Arco
Images/Alamy: 29. Ulrich Baumgarten/varioimages/Alamy: 16. Natalie Behring/Panos: 40.
www.Boots.com: 30. Klaus Oscar Bromberg/Alamy: 12. Marcus Brown/Shutterstock: front cover.
byllwill/istockphoto: 28. Mark Henley/Panos: 17t. David Hills/istockphoto: 14. Image Source/Rex
Features: 9. Jodi Jacobsen/istockphoto: 21. Andy Johnstone/Panos: 24, 27. Yanis Kontos/Panos: 38. Paul
Lowe/Panos: 22. Luoman/istockphoto: 10. Jenny Matthews/Panos: 11. Mikadx/istockphoto: 13. Steve
Morgan/Greenpeace: 33. Michael Morgensen/Panos: 20. Jim Parkin/istockphoto: 25. Giacomo
Pirozzi/Panos: 15, 17b. Abbie Traylor–Smith/Panos: 34. Photograph reproduced with the kind
permission of Marie Stopes International: 39. Chris Stowers/Panos: 26r. Ami Vitale/Panos: 36. Kelvin
Wakefield/istockphoto: 19. Felicia Webb/Christian Aid: 41b. Xi Wenbao/MAXPPP/Photoshot: 31.
Graeme Williams/Panos: 41t. Sarah Wilson/Christian Aid: 23. Ariadne van Zandbergen/Alamy: 37.


1213
32010


9 8 7 6 5 4 3 2 1

# Contents

# Population Today

I n 2009, the number of people in the world hit 6.7 billion. This total is set to rise by approximately 2.5 billion people over the next 40 years. Every one of these people will need food to eat and a place to live. Each will also have the right, enshrined in international law, to a standard of living that ensures their health and well-being.

## Sustainable Population Growth

The problem with this level of population growth is that it places great demands on the Earth's resources. This book looks at how the growing human population is linked to the environmental and social challenges we face—something that has implications for how everyone lives—and highlights what is being done to make population growth more sustainable.

"When people can plan their families, they can plan their lives. They can plan to beat poverty. They can plan on healthier mothers and children. They can plan to gain equality for women. Plan to support World Population Day this year!"

From the web site of World Population Day 2008

### Facts

According to the UNFPA (United Nations Population Fund):

- Humans are depleting natural resources, degrading soil and water, and creating waste at an alarming rate, even as new technology raises crop yields, conserves resources, and cleans up pollution.

- Rich nations with low population growth are mainly accountable for the unsustainable use of the planet's resources; developing countries, with lower overall consumption, contribute a growing share of total carbon dioxide ($CO_2$) emissions.

- Slowing the rate of population growth may give countries time to take measures to meet people's needs while protecting the environment through various means.

- Preventing unwanted births through family planning and guaranteeing individuals and couples the right to reproductive health can help slow population growth rates and moderate environmental impact—and it might be one of the most cost-effective ways of doing so.

## Campaign:

## World Population Day

The issue of world population is highlighted every year on July 11. This is World Population Day, which is organized by the UNFPA. World Population Day is held as a way of highlighting the fact that people have a basic human right to decide, freely and responsibly, the number and timing of their children. This goal is highlighted every year, because it provides a vital way in which the challenge of population growth can be tackled.

Today, even though there are many different ways available for people to plan and control the size of their families, hundreds of millions of adults and young people still do not have access to safe and effective birth control. In 2009, World Population Day celebrated its 20th year by focusing on the importance of educating girls. Doing so can help combat poverty and promote human rights and equality between men and women.

# The Population Explosion

**A**bout 2,000 years ago, there were approximately 200 million people on the planet, and it took until about 1800 for the population to reach 1 billion. Then the global population doubled between 1800 and 1930 to reach 2 billion. By 1999, the world's population had swollen to 6 billion people.

## How It Happened

The world's population grew so dramatically in the twentieth century for two main reasons:

- First, people began to live significantly longer as a result of improvements in living standards and developments in medicines, which have cured many infectious diseases, such as cholera and malaria.

- Second, people in many parts of the world continued to have a lot of babies. As each generation had yet more children, so the world's population boomed or exploded.

## Unbalanced Growth

The human population is still growing, but at a rate that is unevenly distributed across the world. It is growing faster in less developed countries (LDCs) than in more developed countries (MDCs). Also, the annual rate of population growth is now falling, from a maximum of about 2.2 percent to about 1.2 percent.

▲ According to the United Nations, by 2050, 86 percent of the world population is expected to live in LDCs such as Brazil.

| Major area | Population (millions) | | | Projected population in 2050 (millions) | | |
|---|---|---|---|---|---|---|
| | *1950* | *1975* | *2007* | *Low* | *Medium* | *High* |
| World | 2,535 | 4,076 | 6,671 | 7,792 | 9,191 | 10,756 |
| More developed countries | 814 | 1,048 | 1,223 | 1,065 | 1,245 | 1,451 |
| Less developed countries | 1,722 | 3,028 | 5,448 | 6,727 | 7,946 | 9,306 |
| Least developed countries | 200 | 358 | 804 | 1,496 | 1,742 | 2,002 |
| Other less developed countries | 1,521 | 2,670 | 4,644 | 5,231 | 6,204 | 7,304 |
| Africa | 224 | 416 | 965 | 1,718 | 1,998 | 2,302 |
| Asia | 1,411 | 2,394 | 4,030 | 4,444 | 5,266 | 6,189 |
| Europe | 548 | 676 | 731 | 566 | 664 | 777 |
| Latin America and the Caribbean | 168 | 325 | 572 | 641 | 769 | 914 |
| North America | 172 | 243 | 339 | 382 | 445 | 517 |
| Oceania | 13 | 21 | 34 | 42 | 49 | 56 |

Source: Population Division of the Department of Economic and Social Affairs of the United Nations Secretariat (2007). World Population Prospects: The 2006 Revision, Highlights. New York: United Nations.

## MDC Population Growth Trends

In many MDCs, populations are steady or only growing because of immigration. Population growth has slowed in these countries as fertility rates have fallen. Women have stopped having so many babies largely as a result of wider use of contraception (see pages 36–39) and a reduction in the economic need to have lots of children. Women are also more economically active than they used to be, and this leads them to get married and have children later.

## LDC Population Growth Trends

In most LDCs, fertility rates remain high, largely because contraceptives are not as readily available, but also because there are still many economic and social pressures on women to have large families. For this reason, in many LDCs women still have four or more babies. The combination of a high birth rate, higher life expectancy, and a lower death rate is continuing the world's population explosion. Almost all future population growth is expected to be in LDCs— where many of the most fragile habitats and wildlife environments exist.

## How Many People Will There Be?

It is now thought that the rate of population growth will continue to fall around the world as family planning education spreads and people are given the means to control their fertility. Some experts believe that population growth will stop altogether. The United Nations Population Division has made a number of projections that show that by 2050, there will be between about 7.8 billion and 10.8 billion people on Earth.

▼ **Pregnant women wait at a health care facility in Ethiopia.**

"The key problem facing humanity in the coming century is how to bring a better quality of life—for 8 billion or more people—without wrecking the environment entirely in the attempt."

Edward O. Wilson, scientist

# People and the Planet

The billions of people who live on Earth are now having a massive combined impact on the environment. Among the key environmental problems caused by people are the following:

- The destruction, fragmentation, or change of animal and plant habitats. Key habitats under threat from human activities such as farming, fishing, and logging include forests, coral reefs, and wetlands.

- The pollution of the air and water. Many scientists are particularly worried about carbon dioxide emissions caused by humans burning fossil fuels, such as coal and oil. It is thought that these are causing significant changes in the Earth's climate that could harm animals and plants and damage their habitats.

- The depletion of non-renewable natural resources, such as oil, and the overuse of other resources, such as water.

- The introduction of invasive species into wild areas through human activity. These species compete with the natural animals and plants and can ultimately kill them off.

## Biodiversity and People in Peril

One important measure of the health of the environment is biodiversity. Many scientists now believe that the Earth is facing a catastrophic loss of biodiversity and that human activity is responsible. For example, many experts believe that more than 20 percent of the world's mammals are threatened with extinction.

Environmental destruction is bad for the planet and bad for people. As we use up the Earth's resources, it becomes more difficult for people to find food, get the water they need to drink, and get the resources they need to lead their lives. The poor are particularly at risk, as they cannot simply buy their way out of the problem.

## Debate: Earth in Overshoot

The impact of human beings on the planet is now thought to exceed the Earth's capability to regenerate. It is thought that globally, 1.4 Earths' worth of resources are used in one year. But some countries place greater demands on the Earth's resources than others. A conservation group called the Global Footprint Network (GFN) has figured out how much of the world's resources each country uses. Here is how many Earths we would need if everyone lived like a resident of the following countries:

- United States of America—5.4 Earths
- Canada—4.2 Earths
- United Kingdom—3.1 Earths
- Germany—2.5 Earths
- Italy—2.2 Earths
- South Africa—1.4 Earths
- Argentina—1.2 Earths
- Costa Rica—1.1 Earths

In comparison, if everyone lived like a resident of India, we would need only 0.4 Earths to meet everyone's annual requirements.

According to the GFN, one day we don't want to celebrate is Earth Overshoot Day (when humanity begins living beyond its ecological means). This day creeps earlier every year because we are using resources faster than they are being replenished. The GFN has calculated that humanity has been in overshoot since the mid-1980s, when the first Earth Overshoot Day fell on December 31, 1986. By 2009, it had moved earlier by about 14 weeks, to September 25.

What do you think could be done to push forward Earth Overshoot Day? How easy do you think it would be to implement your measures on a local and global scale?

"Humans now require the resources of 1.4 planets. Just like any company, nature has a budget—it can only produce so many resources and absorb so much waste each year. Globally, we now demand the biological capacity of 1.4 planets . . . but, of course, we only have one."

Global Footprint Network web site

AVAILABLE RESOURCES

0%    100%

OVERSHOOT

140%

▶ In 2008, the worldwide population used 140 percent of the yearly supply of sustainably available resources.

▲ Rain forest deforestation in South America is one of the more obvious forms of habitat destruction.

# Global Footprints

The world's human population is having a dramatic effect on the environment. But people around the world have vastly different individual impacts on the planet. A person's impact is known as their ecological "footprint." The size of this footprint depends on many different factors. Among the most important are these:

**The amount a person consumes:** People consume food, fuel, water, clothes, and many other resources and manufactured goods. An affluent (rich) person can consume a lot more products and resources (often obtained from countries far away from the places they live) than a poor person. This, in turn, means they are responsible for a lot more of the environmental destruction, waste, and pollution that is produced when things are produced, manufactured, used, and thrown away.

**The technology a person uses:** People can reduce their environmental impact by using environmentally friendly technology, such as energy-efficient heating systems.

**The choices people make and the things they do:** People can also reduce their ecological footprint by behaving in environmentally friendly ways, such as recycling, riding a bicycle instead of driving a car, or eating food produced in an environmentally friendly way.

▼ **Growing our own food in a garden like this—in an environmentally friendly way—is just one thing we can do to reduce our ecological footprint.**

"If our demands on the planet continue at the same rate, by the mid-2030s, we will need the equivalent of two planets to maintain our lifestyles."
James P. Leape, Director-General, WWF International

## Ecological Responsibility

People around the world have different ways of life and standards of living. This affects the impact that individual countries have on the environment. For example, World Wildlife Fund calculates that even though high-income countries (such as the United States and Britain) only have 15 percent of the world's population, they account for about 36 percent of humanity's total ecological footprint. This shows that the environmental impact of the human population is not just the number of people who are consuming resources, putting pressure on the environment, and producing pollution and waste; it is also how much each person consumes and how much other ecological damage they are responsible for.

## Case Study: Living Alongside Nature

As populations rise, pressure on the environment will grow. This is a particularly pressing problem in LDCs, where populations are rising fastest. Many environmentalists are now arguing that the rich countries of the world should help LDCs protect their natural environment to help them cope with this challenge.

In 2008, the Congo Basin Forest Fund (CBFF) was set up to do just this. The Congo Basin rain forest is the second largest in the world. It is home to an incredible diversity of life and also helps provide a livelihood for tens of millions of people. Despite this, it is being rapidly destroyed.

The CBFF has been set up to help local communities find ways of making a living that do not harm the rain forest and that provide an alternative to logging, mining, felling trees, and destructive farming. So far, Britain and Norway are providing more than $160 million to the project.

▶ Mbuti children hunt in a traditional, sustainable way in the Congo Basin Forest in Cameroon.

1

# Population Challenge: Sustainable Growth

There are two main ways in which the negative impact people have on the planet can be tackled: reducing consumption and reducing population pressure.

## Impact Reduction

First, the impact of individuals, communities, and organizations can be reduced. We can consume fewer natural resources and produce less pollution and waste. This can be done using technology and through changes that people can make to their lifestyles. This approach is particularly important in MDCs where people consume a lot, especially as the impact of their consumption is felt across the world. However, many LDCs, such as China and India, are increasing their levels of consumption. Using the latest "green technology" can help these countries to develop in ways that cause less harm to the environment.

## Pressure Release

Second, the pressure of population growth can be removed, or populations can actually be reduced, by helping people to have fewer babies. Reducing population pressure is particularly important in LDCs with rapidly expanding populations. Reducing the rapid growth of populations in these countries will make it easier for governments to cope with many environmental problems, such as water shortages, and also make human problems such as poverty more manageable.

To solve the environmental problems facing the world, both approaches are necessary. Many environmental problems would be much worse if some countries, such as China, had not already taken steps to limit the growth in their populations, or if many individuals, companies, and organizations had not already acted to reduce their environmental impact.

▲ These workers are collecting recycling in Germany. People in MDCs must reduce their consumption and the amount of waste they produce.

## Debate: All About Fairness

Think about why some LDCs might want to reduce population growth pressure, and the part that population control and education might play. In what ways do you agree or disagree with the following statement:

"It is unfair to expect poorer people, especially in LDCs, to limit the size of their families when it is the high levels of consumption in richer parts of the world that is driving so much environmental destruction."

## Campaign: Optimum Population Trust—Pushing for a Limit to World Population

The Optimum Population Trust (OPT) believes that Earth may not be able to support more than half its present numbers before the end of this century. It estimates that the sustainable world population is 5.1 billion people. The group campaigns for the stabilization and gradual decrease of the human population on a global level. It argues that such an approach would allow people in LDCs to improve their standard of living while reducing the environmental impact of people in highly populated MDCs, such as Taiwan and South Korea.

▲ A group of women in Kolkata, India, take part in birth control lessons for slum dwellers and homeless people.

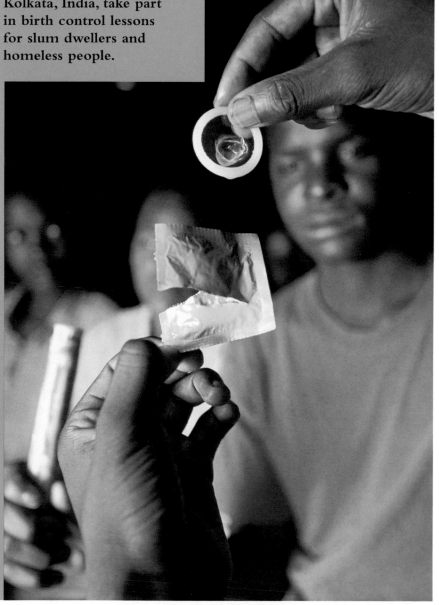

"Both globally and nationally, the population projections are alarming and will clearly put extreme pressure on life-support systems. Fortunately, more and more experts are highlighting the crucial role of human numbers in environmental problems, not least the recent rise in food prices."

David Nicholson-Lord, OPT research associate

◀ A health education talk at a family planning clinic in Zimbabwe. Using condoms is an effective method of preventing HIV/AIDS infection and unplanned pregnancy, but many people do not do so for religious reasons.

# A Place to Live

People need a place to live. Yet housing the world's human population (and building the roads and other infrastructure that people need) has already caused massive amounts of environmental destruction. As populations grow, finding ways to house people in a sustainable way becomes ever more challenging.

▲ This favela in Iporanga, Brazil, has been rebuilt by the Affordable Housing Institute to provide better homes for the expanding urban population.

## Challenges and Opportunities in Cities

One of the most significant global milestones in human history was reached in 2008, when, for the first time ever, more people lived in urban areas than in the countryside. It has been calculated that by 2030, almost 5 billion people will live in towns and cities. This has immense implications for the environment. People living in cities have a massive appetite for resources: energy, food, and water. These "inputs" are brought in from far beyond the boundaries of the cities themselves (often from foreign countries). Cities also produce vast quantities of waste and air and water pollution, which also affect the environment in places far away from the city.

## Calculating a Footprint

According to a recent study of London's ecological footprint called "City Limits," Londoners consumed almost 50 million tons of material, more than 150,000 gigawatt hours of energy, and produced more than 26 million tons of waste each year. The study calculated that London's ecological footprint was 293 times its geographical area.

## City Solutions

However, people in cities do live relatively close together, and this means that there are opportunities for reducing the environmental impact of their citizens. For example, in some Swedish cities, waste heat from industrial factories is used to supply whole districts with "district heating," while other cities, such as Curitiba in Brazil, have pioneered cheap public transportation systems that allow their residents to get around in a relatively environmentally friendly way.

> "A return to well-designed higher-density living, in rural as well as urban areas, can build sustainable communities and secure environmental objectives."
>
> Campaign to Protect Rural England

## Case Study: Saving the Countryside

Britain is an MDC that has already lost a lot of its wildlife areas and biodiversity, especially in the densely populated southeast. However, many parts of the country are still experiencing population growth. This is due partly to immigration from other countries and partly because people move to specific areas of the country where there are jobs. To deal with this population pressure, the government is planning to build a total of 3 million new homes by 2020.

Many conservation groups in the United Kingdom are concerned that such a large increase in homebuilding could threaten the remaining British countryside and cause other environmental problems, such as increased road traffic, pollution, and quarrying. To try to protect the British countryside, the Campaign to Protect Rural England (CPRE) is calling for new housing to be "higher density," so that it takes up less land. They want to stop urban sprawl by persuading the government to make better use of previously developed "brownfield" land and to encourage the regeneration of urban land.

▼ New high-density housing, like this in Leeds, in the United Kingdom, may help to reduce the pressure on the countryside.

# The Impact of Agriculture

**P**eople need food, yet growing food and other crops, raising livestock, and catching fish to feed people has led to widespread habitat destruction—from the loss of wetlands and prairies in the United States to the burning of rain forest in Brazil. Modern agriculture also uses a lot of water and uses vast quantities of fertilizers, pesticides, and other chemicals. The production of these chemicals uses fossil fuels, and their use causes a wide range of pollution problems.

## Food Miles

The impact of farming and its relationship to population and consumption is a complicated one. Many of the foods people eat (especially people in rich countries) are imported from other countries. For example, bananas, coffee, and even mineral water are just some of the foodstuffs imported from abroad. This means that increasing consumption of food by people in one country can have far-reaching environmental consequences in other nations. What is more, the farther that food has to be transported, the more fuel is used and the more pollution and waste is produced. This impact is measured as "food miles." Unfortunately for the environment, the level of food consumption and waste is rising in many countries. At the same time, growing population numbers (either through high birth rates or the migration of people into an area) is often a factor in the growth of agriculture, especially in developing countries. It is thought that food production will have to rise by 50 percent by 2030 to meet increased demand. This means that the challenge of finding ways to feed the world in a sustainable way is getting more urgent all the time.

▼ **Many of the foods and other plant products that people use in MDCs come from plantations in poorer countries, such as this one in Malaysia.**

▲ In many LDCs, the expansion of agriculture is linked to the destruction of rain forests and other key habitats. This leads to the death of many animals, such as the mothers of these young orangutans from Indonesia.

## Campaign: Save the Rain Forest with Your Shopping

The environmental pressure group Friends of the Earth highlighted the global link between the food products we buy and the destruction of the environment in its recent Palm Oil Campaign. According to the group, demand for palm oil, a vegetable oil present in 1 in 10 supermarket products (including chocolate, bread, and potato chips), is the most significant cause of rain forest loss in Malaysia and Indonesia. This, in turn, threatens species such as the orangutan and the Sumatran tiger.

The campaign, which Friends of the Earth carried out with the Ape Alliance, was launched in 2005 and has attracted global attention to the impact of the trade in palm oil. It has also persuaded major supermarkets to join the Roundtable on Sustainable Palm Oil. Friends of the Earth is continuing to campaign to ensure that many supermarkets deliver on their pledge to only use palm oil produced in a sustainable way, which does not lead to rain forest destruction.

"We have achieved a huge amount over the last few years, but the sad fact is that the rain forest in Indonesia and Malaysia continues to be destroyed at an alarming rate, and the orangutan is still gravely threatened. Now the use of palm oil as a biofuel could push the orangutan over the edge. The UK government must ensure no palm oil is imported for use as biofuel."

Friends of the Earth Palm Oil Campaigner, Ed Matthew

**21**

# Why Are People Hungry?

▲ This is a UN World Food Programme distribution point in Sudan. People who are facing famine need food aid, but it cannot sustain people in the long term.

In 2008, there were more than 960 million people in the world who didn't have sufficient safe and nutritious food. About 60 percent of them live in South Asia and sub-Saharan Africa. As the number of people in the developing world increases, and as consumption by the rich increases, this problem is likely to get worse.

## Food Poor

While famines caused by natural disasters, drought, war, and other problems are responsible for many people starving, one of the main reasons that people do not have enough to eat is that they are poor. They do not have enough land to grow the food they need and cannot afford to buy enough to sustain them.

"For millions of people in developing countries, eating the minimum amount of food every day to live an active and healthy life is a distant dream."

Assistant Director-General Hafez Ghanem, presenting *The State of Food Insecurity in the World 2008*

These problems have been exacerbated by the fact that

• Many poor countries do not grow enough food for their populations and rely on imports. If global food prices rise, this can cause immense hardship.

• In many countries, agricultural land has been degraded by wind and water erosion or because it has become waterlogged or salty.

• Many poor countries grow cash crops for export (often to pay international debts). This takes up land that could be used to grow food for local people.

• In recent years, the development of biofuels (fuel made from plants such as corn) has accelerated. This has helped to drive up the cost of food worldwide.

• It is thought by many scientists that man–made climate change is making drought and water shortages more common. This is thought to be having an impact on food production.

## Case Study: Helping Poor Farmers

Local farmers in LDCs are a vital part of the solution to world hunger. However, cheap imported food (sometimes supplied as aid) often makes it difficult for these farmers to compete and make a living. Around the world, many groups are working to help countries achieve "food security"—the ability to meet their food needs themselves.

In Haiti, dairy farmers have found it hard to make a living because of cheap imported milk. Many farmers have left the country or been forced to cut down trees to turn into charcoal to sell.

To help them compete with the cheaper imports, a group called Veterimed (a partner of the aid agency Christian Aid) has set up the Let Agogo (Flowing Milk) dairy. Haitian farmers, like the one below, sell their milk to the dairy, where it is processed into fresh yogurt and pasteurized milk. Then it is delivered to supermarkets, shops, and restaurants in the city. Veterimed also ensures that the benefits reach as many people as possible by funding community projects, such as water pumps and tanks.

According to Christian Aid, such "pro-poor" solutions are a vital part of any drive to feed the world, and they are calling for more to be done by politicians to reform trade rules to protect poor farmers.

# Making Agriculture Sustainable

**S**ustainable agriculture is the term used to describe agriculture that has a minimal impact on the environment. Farmers who practice sustainable agriculture use a wide range of techniques to maintain the health of their soil and to encourage and help wildlife. These include using organic fertilizers rather than man-made chemicals, using natural pest control rather than chemical pesticides, and using water carefully.

## Changing Old Habits

Around the world, many farmers are starting to change the way they act to become more sustainable, often with the support of their governments. It is hoped that the growth in sustainable agriculture will help reduce the environmental impact of feeding the world population's ever-increasing appetite for food.

"Organic agriculture is proving to be a serious contender in modern farming and a more environmentally sustainable system over the long term."

David Suzuki, environmentalist

▼ Women farm workers harvest groundnuts (peanuts) in a field in Andhra Pradesh, India. They have been trained in sustainable farming techniques.

▼ GM wheat is harvested in the United States.

## Debate: Can GM Crops Help?

In the past, more food has been produced by improvements in agriculture and crops. For example, in the 1960s, new strains of food crops, such as IR8 rice, were introduced in countries such as India. These new crops allowed farmers to grow much more food on their land. This was called the "green revolution," and it helped to feed the rapidly growing populations of countries around the world.

Scientists have now succeeded in changing the genetic makeup of food plants in the laboratory to create crops with new characteristics. Such genetically modified (GM) food is one of the most contentious issues in agriculture. Those who support GM crops say that they could be a vital tool in the fight against world hunger. They point to GM crops such as golden rice. This rice plant has been genetically modified to contain a precursor to vitamin A, and it could help to prevent vitamin A-related diseases in children.

Opponents of GM crops, on the other hand, believe that the risks are too great. They fear that such crops could give rise to "super weeds," and they are also concerned about the impact of GM crops on human health and on the livelihoods of poor farmers.

## Case Study: Training Farmers

Aid agencies working in some LDCs are giving farmers the help they need to become more sustainable. For example, Christian Aid is working with the Deccan Development Society (DDS) to train female farmers in the southern Indian state of Andhra Pradesh in sustainable farming techniques.

The DDS has already helped communities in the area to increase their harvests by up to six times using manure, compost, and crops that can absorb extra nitrogen into the soil from the air.

The DDS works with women's groups (or "sanghams") in about 75 villages. The group helps them to become self-sufficient producers of organic food, to diversify their crops, and to influence local and state government policies. The 5,000 members of these sanghams are among the poorest in the community, and most of them are "dalits," the most excluded group in India's social hierarchy. According to Christian Aid, through their collective efforts, the women have turned 5,000 acres of wasteland into productive cropland that now feeds their families and 50,000 of the poorest people in their communities as well.

# Not Enough to Drink?

Of all the resource use issues facing the world, it may be water that will be the one that poses the biggest challenge. People cannot live without water, and they need water to keep clean and healthy. Water is also vital for growing food. In many countries, water is already in short supply. Many of these countries are also ones with rapidly growing populations.

## Water Stress

According to the UNFPA, in the year 2000, 508 million people lived in 31 water-stressed or water-scarce countries. By 2025, 3 billion people will be living in 48 such countries. In these countries—many of which are in sub-Saharan Africa and the Middle East—water is often in short supply or not available, making it difficult to produce enough food and forcing people to walk many miles to get water to drink.

## Case Study: Los Angeles Water Saving

Water scarcity is not just an issue for LDCs. For example, Los Angeles, California (which has a rapidly growing population), is struggling to get enough water. In such places, water conservation is vital to protect the surrounding countryside, from which vast quantities of water are taken. To save water, people in Los Angeles are encouraged to limit the amount of water they use for jobs, such as lawn irrigation, and to install water-saving devices, such as ultra-low-flush toilets. In recent years, nearly 1.3 million of these toilets were installed.

▼ This is the Los Angeles water treatment plant.

▼ Drinking water is sold from the back of a tanker in India.

"Worldwide, 54 percent of the annual available freshwater is being used. If consumption per person remains steady, by 2025 we could be using 70 percent of the total because of population growth alone."

UNFPA State of World Population Report

## Case Study: Helping Communities Get the Water They Need

Practical Action is a development charity that works with some of the poorest people on Earth. In Sri Lanka, a country that has suffered from prolonged drought and that has a growing population, the group works with local people to implement low-cost "rainwater harvesting" technology that uses tanks to collect and store rainwater that is channeled by gutters and pipes as it runs off the roofs of houses.

Practical Action aims to create a local skills base among builders and users of the tanks, so that communities can manage their own rainwater-harvesting programs. The community of Muthukandiya is one that has already benefited. According to the group, two local masons in the region received several days of on-the-job training in building the 1,321 gallon (5,000 L) household storage tanks. Thanks to the project, 37 families in and around Muthukandiya have storage tanks. These households have considerably more water than households that rely on wells. Their water is much cleaner, too.

▲ This water storage tank is in a village in Sri Lanka. It ensures a reliable source of drinking water for the community.

## Continuing Challenge

In MDCs, water shortages are often caused by the fact that people use a lot of water. For example, a person in North America can use more than 35 times as much water as a person in sub-Saharan Africa.

The water crisis is set to get more challenging as populations in water-stressed countries increase. Many scientists also think that climate change will make droughts and water shortages more frequent.

# Too Many People Using too Much

The world's growing population consumes vast quantities of resources. Some of these resources, including fuels such as oil, coal, and gas, are what is known as "nonrenewable." This means that there is only a limited amount of them available. The consumption of these resources is on the rise in MDCs and in countries with emerging economies, such as China and India. Many people are worried that, with the continuing rise in demand and the growing world population, we are in danger of running out of some nonrenewable energy sources, particularly oil.

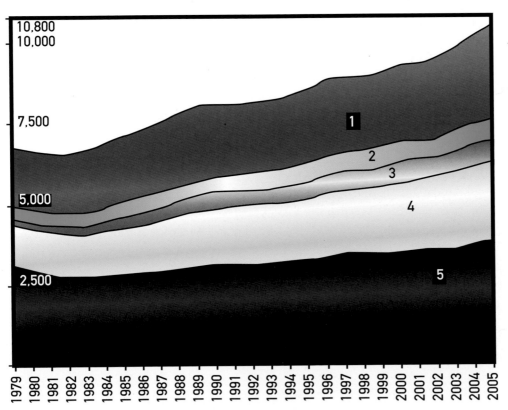

▲ Solar panels are just one renewable technology that could help supply nonpolluting energy to the world's growing population.

◀ This graph shows total world energy resource consumption from 1979 to 2005 in millions of metric tons oil equivalent.

1. Coal consumption
2. Hydroelectricity consumption
3. Nuclear energy consumption
4. Gas consumption
5. Oil consumption

## Kicking the Oil Habit

Oil is one of the most important resources that people use. It powers cars, heats homes, and is also used to produce chemicals in some medicines, industry, and agriculture. In many ways, oil makes it possible for us to live a modern life. But many scientists believe that we are already pumping the maximum amount of oil from the ground, and that world production of oil will reduce in years to come as supplies run out.

## New Thinking

Around the world, governments are waking up to the fact that we must reduce our dependence on oil and other nonrenewable fuels. For example, when he came to power in 2009, U.S. president Barack Obama set out a plan to move the country in this direction. Its aim was that within 10 years, the United States would save more oil than it currently imports. Among the projects the plan outlined were these:

• Putting 1 million plug-in hybrid cars—cars that can get up to 150 miles per gallon—on the road by 2015.

• Ensuring that 10 percent of America's electricity comes from renewable sources (such as wind, wave, and solar power) by 2012, and 25 percent by 2025.

▼ Stocks of blue crabs are threatened by growing human demands.

It is hoped that similar "green" technology, renewable energy, and energy-efficiency projects will help supply the energy needs of the world's growing population in a more environmentally friendly way.

## Renewable Resources in Trouble

It is not just nonrenewable resources that are in danger of running out. Some resources that can be naturally replaced, such as wood and soil, are in danger of being overexploited and lost. One key example of a renewable resource in danger is fish. About 1 billion people depend on fish as their main source of protein. However, it is estimated that about half of all fish stocks are being fished at the limits of sustainability. Around the world, fish catches are declining. This is a key challenge to the world's poorest countries with the fastest-growing populations, as many of these are particularly dependent on fish for food.

Many groups are now working to halt the decline of world fish stocks. For example, the WWF helps communities around the world to catch fish in a more sustainable way. In the Philippines, a country with a high rate of population growth and where fish stocks are threatened with overfishing and habitat destruction, the WWF is developing management and enforcement plans to safeguard the Western Visayas Blue Crab Fishery.

"We will harness the sun and the winds and the soil to fuel our cars and run our factories."

Barack Obama's Inaugural Presidential Address

# People and Pollution

The more people there are, the greater the challenge to clean up the pollution and waste they are responsible for—whether it is the garbage they throw away, the air pollution from the power plants that generate the electricity they use, or the sewage they produce when they use the bathroom. Pollution is a particular challenge when there are lots of people in one place, such as a city or resort.

## Two Pollution Perspectives

In MDCs, great strides have been made to clean up the environment through tough antipollution laws and through technological improvements. However, many pollution challenges remain, including the problem of global warming (see pages 32–33).

## Case Study: Reducing the Waste Problem

The United Kingdom is a densely populated country, and every year it produces about 331 million tons (300 million t) of waste. One way to reduce the amount of waste people produce is to cut down on packaging, and many companies have come under increasing pressure from consumers to do so. As a result of this pressure and encouragement from the government, the United Kingdom's leading retailers have dramatically cut the number of plastic bags they hand out at checkouts. According to the UK-based organization WRAP (the Waste & Resources Action Programme), retailers have reduced the number of plastic bags they give out from 13.4 billion in 2006 to 9.9 billion in 2008. They have also increased the recycled content of the bags and reduced their weight. The government's long-term aim is to cut the amount of household waste buried in landfills by 50 percent per person by 2020.

▶ Boots' Botanics products feature reusable containers, packaging made from recycled materials, and minimal packaging.

In many rapidly industrializing countries, pollution is a critical problem. In China, for example, factories and power plants with inadequate pollution cleanup technology are polluting the country's air and water, causing many health and environmental problems. Sewage is another key problem in many LDCs, where a lack of basic sanitation threatens people's health.

"The fact that toilets are at the bottom of politicians' lists is outrageous when you consider that 5,000 children [in LDCs] die every day from lack of basic sanitation."

Steve Cockburn, of the End Water Poverty (EWP) Campaign

## Case Study: Olympic Cleanup

The challenge of cleaning up air pollution in China was highlighted in the run-up to the 2008 Olympic Games, which were held in the country's capital city of Beijing. To make sure that the city's air was clean enough for the games to take place, a large number of steps were taken to reduce pollutants such as sulfur dioxide, nitrogen dioxide, particulates, and carbon monoxide. These steps included removing millions of vehicles from the city's streets and closing down factories. Billions of dollars were invested to clean the air, and the number of "blue sky" days increased from 100 in 1998 to 246 in 2007. Days with an Air Pollution Index (API) of 100 or less are blue sky days.

Before the Olympic Games, there were still concerns for the health of athletes taking part in what has been one of the world's most polluted cities. However, the air quality during the games was good enough to allow the athletes to compete. After the Olympic Games, air pollution in Beijing remains an issue; however, it is hoped that the games have provided a jump-start to the country's push to clean up the air that its people have to breathe.

▼ The introduction of these environmentally friendly buses in Beijing are part of China's push to reduce pollution levels.

# A Warmer Future?

**M**any scientists think that the Earth's climate is being changed by man-made emissions of greenhouse gases. The most important of these gases is carbon dioxide ($CO_2$), which is produced when fossil fuels such as coal, oil, and gas are burned. It is thought that man-made climate change will lead to an increase in global temperatures, rising sea levels, and other environmental changes that will harm wildlife and people.

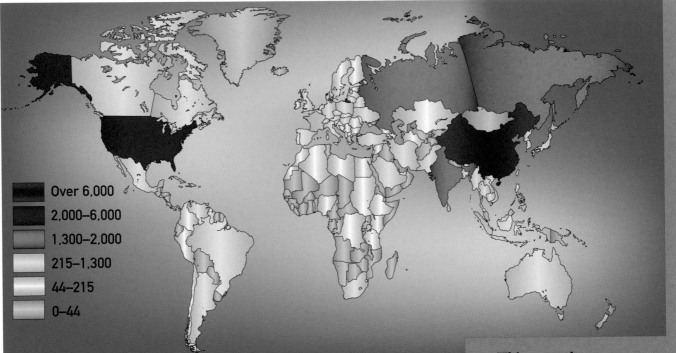

Over 6,000
2,000–6,000
1,300–2,000
215–1,300
44–215
0–44

▲ This map shows current greenhouse gas emissions by country in million tons $CO_2$ equivalent.

## Population Link

The climate change challenge is closely linked to the issue of population growth and over-consumption. Most of the global greenhouse gas emissions come from MDCs. For example, the United States, with about 4.5 percent of the world population, produces more than 20 percent of all $CO_2$ gas emissions. The average American is responsible for about 22 tons (20 t) of $CO_2$ emissions. The average person from India is responsible for just over 1 ton.

At the same time, many of the developing countries that have rising populations are going to be hardest hit by the problems that could be caused by climate change. In particular, it is thought that agriculture in these countries will be badly affected and that it will become more difficult for people to grow the food they need.

As the populations of developing countries such as India grow, and as their economies become more industrialized, so will their emissions of global warming gases rise. It is hoped that developing countries will be able to bypass the global warming problem by installing green technology that does not contribute significantly to climate change.

## Helping Poor Countries Cope

With a population of more than 145 million living in an area the size of New York State, Bangladesh is the most densely populated agrarian country in the world. Because Bangladesh is a low-lying country, it would be very badly affected by any sea level rises caused by climate change.

Nongovernmental organizations (NGOs), such as Christian Aid, are working with the very poorest communities in Bangladesh to help them adapt, prepare, and increase their resilience to the changes that it is thought climate change will bring. These changes include rising water levels and more "extreme" weather. This is being done through measures such as raising homes, roads, and public places and building cyclone shelters. Christian Aid is also assisting in the development of secure and sustainable livelihoods so that people are better able to plan for and recover more quickly from disaster.

"Warming of the climate system is unequivocal, as is now evident from observations of increases in global average air and ocean temperatures, widespread melting of snow and ice, and rising global average sea level."

Intergovernmental Panel on Climate Change

## Campaign: What's Being Done?

Industrialized countries have made commitments to reduce the amount of global warming gases they produce. Steps are now being taken in many of these countries to make industry, transportation, housing, and power generation less polluting. However, many people do not think that enough is being done, and this has led to protests by environmental groups such as Greenpeace. For example, in 2009, more than 2,500 clean energy activists came to Washington, D.C., and, successfully shut all entrances to the coal-fired Capitol Power Plant, which is used to heat and cool the Capitol building. Plans were already in place to switch the plant to cleaner-burning natural gas, however, the protest showed popular suport for combating climate change.

▲ A campaigner makes his point wearing a polar bear suit. Polar bears are at risk as rising temperatures melt more ice in the Arctic.

# Population and People

**P**opulation growth isn't just an environmental issue. It also has a massive impact on people's standard of living and their health. What's more, population growth is making it more difficult for many countries to lift people out of poverty and this, in turn, makes it more difficult for them to deal with the environmental problems they face.

## The Impact on People

Populations in many developing countries are still growing, because women continue to have large numbers of children. This affects people in many ways, including the following:

• Population growth makes it more difficult for countries to cope with natural and man-made disasters, such as famines and wars.

• It affects women's health and well-being. In many countries, health care is poor or not readily available. More than half a million women die during childbirth or due to pregnancy complications each year.

• Having larger families can make it more difficult for parents to provide adequate nutrition to all their children. It also makes it more difficult for them to provide care and schooling, especially for girls.

• A growing population makes it harder for governments to provide schools, hospitals, and other vital services, such as sanitation and water supplies.

• Increasing population pressure is driving the development of dangerous and unhealthy slums around towns and cities.

## Population and Poverty

According to the UNFPA, population growth has a significant effect on poverty in many countries. The organization highlights a study of 48 countries, which estimates that the proportion of people living in poverty would have fallen by a third if the birth rate had fallen by 5 per 1,000 people in the 1980s.

▲ Many poor families, like this one in Bangladesh, do not have access to education and contraceptives, leading to unsustainable population growth.

## Demographic Window

Reducing population growth can also help countries get themselves out of poverty because it can open up what is known as a "demographic window of opportunity." If the birth rate in a country drops, then there is a time during which the number of people of working age grows relative to the number of people they must work to support.

In 2001, the United Nations established the Millennium Development Goals—crucial targets for improving the environment and people's livelihoods. Many people now think that meeting these goals will be impossible if population growth in developing countries is not slowed down.

"In many regions, the Millennium Development Goals are not attainable without greater focus on slowing population growth, through making voluntary family planning universally accessible, and empowering women to access reproductive health services."

The UK Government's All Party Parliamentary Group on Population, Development, and Reproductive Health

# Reducing Population Growth

**A**lthough population growth is acknowledged as a key underlying factor behind many environmental and social problems, the challenge of reducing population growth is a complex one.

▼ **At this Marie Stopes health care clinic in Nairobi, Kenya, women receive welfare information and support.**

## Enforced Planning

Many countries have tried to reduce their populations using targets, laws, and regulations. For example, in the 1970s, India implemented a family-planning program in which people were paid or forced to be sterilized. In China, a one-child policy was set up in 1979. This meant that much of the urban population was only allowed to have one child. Although programs such as these have reduced population growth, they have been criticized as being unfair.

## Support and Education

Today, most people—from governments and doctors to charities and individuals—think that the best approach to tackling population growth is to focus on giving people the information, support, and education they need to make choices about having babies and to help them improve their reproductive health. This approach not only helps people limit the size of their families, it also helps prevent women from dying in childbirth.

## Campaign: Interact Worldwide

One group that works in this way is Interact Worldwide. This group works in some of the poorest countries and settings in the world. Its aim is to improve the sexual and reproductive health and rights of those people who are often forgotten by the rest of society, such as those living with HIV, rural women, adolescents, and refugees. For example, it campaigns for universal access to condoms, which not only prevent women from getting pregnant, but also guard against many diseases. Despite this, according to Interact Worldwide, the majority of people in LDCs still find it difficult to access the condoms they need.

## Case Study:
## Conservation and Contraception

The importance of reducing population growth to the success of environmental protection is widely acknowledged. Because of this, many conservation groups are now incorporating family planning advice in their environmental projects.

For example, in Madagascar's Spiny Forest, the WWF has set up a Population, Health, and Environment Program. The forest is one of Madagascar's most threatened areas. It is also home to an amazing diversity of wildlife and, according to the WWF, almost 100 percent of its plant species are found nowhere else in the world. One of the underlying causes of forest destruction in the region is population growth. Increases in the local population have forced people to use the forest for firewood, agriculture, and other destructive purposes.

According to WWF, their project, which was set up after the group had worked in the region for almost 10 years, aims to address these linked problems by "building community awareness of family planning options, providing counseling and access to contraceptives, and simultaneously initiating sound natural resources management practices and sustainable livelihood strategies."

▼ In Madagascar's Spiny Forest, conservation and population growth are being tackled alongside one another.

"In line with the goals of the International Conference on Population and Development (ICPD), we focus not on numbers, but on each individual's right to a healthy life. Our vision is a world where exercising the right to sexual and reproductive health contributes to the reduction of poverty and a better quality of life." Interact Worldwide, one of the leading groups working on the population issue

# Helping People Plan Their Families

People cannot control the number of children they have without access to effective methods of contraception. Sex education, which teaches people—both men and women—how to use contraception properly and how to safeguard their sexual health, is also vital if people are to plan their families effectively.

## Universal Access

Easy access to reliable and affordable contraceptives and sex education is one of the key reasons for the drop in fertility that has taken place in many countries around the world. For example, according to Interact Worldwide, in Iran, universal access to health care and family planning services has helped bring about a drop in the population growth rate of about 2.4 percent between 1986 and 2004.

▲ This couple and their baby daughter live in Tehran, Iran. Access to effective contraceptives and advice on how to use them give people the choice to plan their families and their lives.

## Progress Problems

However, there are still at least 200 million women who do not have access to safe and effective family planning methods and information. In some countries, there are still religious and cultural reasons why contraceptives are not widely available; in other countries, the resources are not available to provide this vital service at a price people can afford. According to UNFPA, universal access to family planning could save the lives of about 175,000 women each year. This is mainly because so many women in LDCs die in childbirth. UNFPA also says that increasing birth intervals to three years could prevent the deaths of 1.8 million children under the age of five.

## Case Study:
## Midwives on Motorbikes

One of the big family planning problems that people in LDCs have is access to both contraceptives and reproductive health advice. This is partly because many people live far away from towns and hospitals. Marie Stopes International, one of the world's leading family planning charities, is tackling this problem in East Timor, in Southeast Asia. Marie Stopes International has put in place a pilot outreach project, affectionately known as "Midwives on Motorbikes."

According to the group, the project's team of midwives uses motorbikes to travel around the country, often on unpaved roads and through mountain passes, to get basic family planning services and information to distant communities. The group is very proud of the fact that in their first year on the road, the midwives have reached nearly 5,000 people through community information and awareness-raising sessions and activities.

The program has reached hundreds of people who had previously not used contraceptives, and who had limited knowledge of family planning and the dangers of sexually transmitted diseases.

"I walked from 6 a.m. to get here—it has taken me four hours. I have nine children, one of whom died. I brought four of my children with me today, and I've come because I am happy with the help I get from Mary Stopes."

A woman who came to get help from Midwives on Motorbikes

▶ The Midwives on Motorbikes project brings family planning help to people who would otherwise not be able to get it.

**39**

# A Global Challenge

The world's human population is responsible for a wide range of environmental problems, many of which also affect the quality of life that people can enjoy. The world's population is growing and, at the same time, many countries, such as China, are developing rapidly. This will create immense challenges in the future.

## Achieving Sustainable Growth?

The growth rate in the world's population is slowing down as more and more people limit the size of their families. At the same time, people all around the world are working to find ways to reduce the amount of environmental damage human activity is responsible for. Both of these developments are crucial to the preservation of the natural world and to the well-being of future generations.

▼ **Women wait to receive prenatal care in a refugee camp clinic on the border of Ethiopia and the Sudan.**

## A Population Bomb?

The impact of population growth has been the subject of intense study. In the 1960s, Paul Erlich published *The Population Bomb*, in which he argued that overpopulation would lead to mass starvation and that something needed to be done to limit population.

While technology and improvements in agriculture have done a lot to reduce the impact of population growth and to feed people, many people believe that Erlich was right to highlight population as a major problem that needs urgent action. Whether population growth today leads to disasters similar to those he described depends on how people act today and in the future.

## Getting to the Root of the Problem

One of the most fundamental ways of reducing population growth is to improve people's livelihoods and education. This gives people more opportunities and means that they are not so dependent on their children for their well-being. This is particularly true for women in LDCs, who have often been excluded from education and the workplace.

▶ **The work of these children helps their parents, but denies them an education.**

"Girls' and women's education is just as important in reducing birth rates as supplying contraception."

Sadia Chowdhury, senior reproductive and child health specialist at the World Bank

◀ Classes, such as this one, were set up in Afghanistan by Christian Aid to provide education to women in the community.

## A Way Forward?

Vocational training programs for women represent one of the ways forward. These are already being run across the world, by organizations such as Christian Aid. For example, in Afghanistan, where women are often denied education, a project has helped many gain new skills and independence. One woman who attended the course is now able to earn $100 a month as a trainer. She is able to feed her children and has bought a motorbike for her husband. He uses it to drive his wife to literacy classes, so that she can continue her education. Her focus is now on being a good teacher, and she wants to limit the size of her family so that she can keep up her standard of living.

# Glossary

**biodiversity:** the variety of plants, animals, and other forms of life that exist in a certain place

**brownfield land:** an area of land that has previously been used for industrial, commercial, or other development, for example, land where there used to be factories or where there are derelict houses

**carbon dioxide ($CO_2$):** a gas that naturally occurs in the Earth's atmosphere. Carbon dioxide is released when fossil fuels, such as coal, oil, and gas, are burned.

**climate change:** long-term, significant change in the world's climate. Many scientists now believe that man-made greenhouse gases, such as carbon dioxide, are responsible for climate change.

**condom:** a condom is a type of contraceptive. It is an elastic sheath that is rolled onto the penis and physically blocks the passage of sperm.

**contraceptives:** tools used to prevent pregnancy. Contraceptives include condoms, pills, IUDs, and hormone injections.

**ecological footprint:** a measure of the environmental impact of a person or activity in terms of the amount of natural resources they use and the amount of pollution they produce

**famine:** A famine occurs when there is a widespread lack of food and people go hungry.

**fertility:** the ability to have children

**food security:** refers to how safe the supply of food is to a person, household, or even nation. When people do not live in fear of hunger, they can be said to be "food secure."

**fossil fuels:** fuels made from carbon and hydrocarbons, including fuels such as coal, gas, and oil

**genetically modified (GM):** A genetically modified organism is a living thing that has had its genetic makeup changed directly.

**global warming:** an increase in the average measured temperature of the Earth. Many scientists now believe that man-made greenhouse gases, such as carbon dioxide, are responsible for global warming.

**immigration:** the movement of people from one country to another. People become immigrants for many reasons, but often to search for work, education, or a new place to live.

**less developed countries (LDCs):** nations with a low level of economic development

**midwife:** a health care professional who provides help to a woman before, during, and after the birth of her child

**more developed countries (MDCs):** countries that have high levels of economic development

**nonrenewable:** a natural resource that cannot be replaced naturally when it is used

**optimum:** the best possible result

**population:** the number of people who live in a particular region or area

**rain forest:** a forest that is characterized by the high rainfalls that it receives

**rainwater harvesting:** the gathering and storing of rainwater

**regeneration:** renewing or rebuilding a particular place or community

**renewable:** a natural resource that is replenished by natural processes

**reproductive:** anything to do with the conception and birth of new living things

**sex education:** any education about sexual reproduction and relationships and other related issues

**sterilized:** relating to someone who is unable to have children because their reproductive organs have been altered by surgery

**sustainable:** something that can continue to take place without causing lasting damage to the environment

**urban:** relating to a town or city

# Web Sites

U.S. Census
**www.census.gov/main/www/popclock.html**
Take a look at current estimates of populations in the United States and around the world.

United Nations Population Fund
**www.unfpa.org/wpd/index.html**
Find out more about World Population Day and the United Nations Population Fund.

WWF
**www.panda.org/about_our_earth/all_
publications/living_planet_report**
Get the full details about people's impact on the planet from the WWF's Living Planet Report.

Global Footprint Network
**www.footprintnetwork.org/en/index.php**
Find out more about the Global Footprint Network and the impact of different countries on the environment.

Congo Basin Forest Fund
**www.cbf-fund.org**
Find out what the world is doing to help save the Congo Basin Forest.

Optimum Population Trust
**www.optimumpopulation.org**
Find out about the Optimum Population Trust and why its members think the world's population should be reduced.

Campaign to Protect Rural England
**www.cpre.org.uk**
Find out more about the Campaign to Protect Rural England.

Friends of the Earth International
**www.foei.org**
Take a look at the web site of the world's largest grassroots environmental network.

Greenpeace
**www.greenpeace.org**
See what Greenpeace is doing to protect and conserve the environment.

Marie Stopes International
**www.mariestopes.org**
Marie Stopes International works on reproductive issues in 40 countries. Find out what the organization does here.

Interact Worldwide
**www.interactworldwide.org**
See how Interact Worldwide works on issues of sexual and reproductive health and HIV/AIDS.

Christian Aid
**www.christianaid.org.uk**
Find out more about Christian Aid's work to expose and battle the scandal of poverty.

Practical Action
**www.practicalaction.org**
Practical Action believes that the right idea—however small—can change lives. Find out more about its work online.

Please note: Every effort has been made by the publishers to ensure that these web sites contain no inappropriate or offensive material. However, because of the nature of the Internet, it is impossible to guarantee that the contents of these sites will not be altered. We strongly advise that Internet access is supervised by a responsible adult.

# Index